50 ways to confidently improve your business website.

"A guide to squeezing the most out of the internet and how to be confident in knowing what to ask for and what to avoid when dealing with website designers and media companies."

 **Checklist included.**

Stuart Lovatt

ISBN-10: 148019140X
ISBN-13: 978-1480191402

"Stay ahead of the competition, now and in years to come."

INTRODUCTION

"They say you learn from your mistakes, but you don't have to make the same mistakes I made, over my 14 years of business website building."

The world of internet marketing can be a very perilous place for many business owners wanting to make the most of the new electronic economy. As with any other industry, there are charlatans and companies who want to take advantage of less technically savvy people.

The eco-system which is the website marketing world has also to deal with an ever-changing and fast developing set of standards as modern search engines such as Google, Bing and Yahoo continue to evolve and improve their results.

As a business owner, it has never been more important to source a good person or company to work on your website development. Website standards which may have created a successful website two, five or even ten years ago, will not work today and many web professionals have fallen foul of those changes.

You could source out of the millions of website designers, search engine optimisation companies and self-help guides which inhabit the internet today, but it is still a gamble with your business's future.

ASSESS YOUR WEBSITE

"Before making any technical changes to your website, you must assess your current website before entering the search engine arena. Our 'Take Control' checklist at the back of this book will help you to assess your current staff/webmasters/outsourced company's knowledge and abilities so far."

Vanity kills websites

The information contained within this book has been compiled through many years of trial and error and long-term testing.

The first lesson is to look at your website objectively. Take off the rose-tinted spectacles and look at your website through your visitor's eyes.

The most common mistake made by website owners is vanity. Trying to outdo your competitors with an 'all singing and all dancing websites' will impress some people, but you could lose more potential clients than you gain. Taste is subjective. From my experience, an over-designed website will lead to other penalties with the search engines which are detailed in this book.

Search engines are smarter than you think

You may think that the visitors to your site are YOUR visitors, YOUR hits. The truth is, they're not. They are the search engine's visitors and they allow THEIR visitors to visit your website at their discretion.

No search engine has an obligation to direct its traffic to your website. In order to receive a larger volume of their users, you have to gain their trust. You have to show them that your website meets their basic standards and more importantly, prove to them that your website is what people like.

The goalposts which the search engines put in place, through their algorithms and standards, are continually changing. Impressing visitors is only half of the requirements of a truly successful website.

There are a million possible reasons why most websites fail the search engines' standards, but most can be listed for four main reasons:

- Wrong people.
- Wrong advice.
- Poor implementation.
- Stagnant or lack of growth.

Admitting you currently have a problem is the first stage of your website's future recovery or success.

CHANGE IS GOOD

"Search engines are continually changing and changing their algorithms. Your website needs to be responsive to these changes. If your webmaster or the outsource company responsible for the care of your website has no strategy for continually updating the website, then alarm bells should be ringing."

Mapping a route forward

When it comes to websites, change is good, even when it is bad.

To use an analogy, if you are travelling in a car to a destination and you get lost, you have to acknowledge that you are lost before you can change course. If you continue without recognizing your error, you will find yourself even more lost and more time will be wasted.

The same is true with websites. Making changes and monitoring their effects is how a good professional web designer works.

Steering your website to the number one spot on the search engines takes continued alterations, assessment and patience.

Site monitoring

Do you know how many 'unique hits' your website averages? Do you know your 'bounce rate' and 'most excited' web page'?

The good analytical software is essential to let you know if your website is achieving or improving. To be without this information is to be driving blind.

Google's Analytics service, if you are not already using this, is a good place to start. Because of the way it gathers data, it is not entirely accurate, so always use a secondary, more accurate Analytics software through your hosting provider. 'AW Stats' or 'Open Analytics' are common.

Keep your eye on the data, and let your website person/webmaster know you are making use of their efforts.

Patience

You or your webmaster must keep detailed records of changes made. Because of the slow nature of the search engines, changes made today may take 3-6 months to take effect, so knowing what changes you did make will come in handy if you need to 'backpedal' any of them.

There are no quick ways to reach search engine pole position, but if done correctly, then your steady rise through the ranks will be long-lasting and rewarding.

WEBSITE LOAD SPEED

"Considered by most website designers as a minimum requirement, I can tell you from experience that getting your website to load under the 1.5 seconds time frame will not only impress the search engines but most importantly, keep your users happy."

Big is beautiful, but not a sprinter

Modern search engines are on a quest to speed up the internet. The days of slow-loading websites are numbered. If a search engine user's experience is spoiled by a slow-loading website, then this reflects badly on the search engine that sends them there. So your website is currently being monitored. The three 'issues' that people with a slow loading website are:

- Higher bounce rate. (Users returning to the search engine)
- Poor user experience.
- Poor conversion rates.

Many website designers/developers, sitting in their comfortable, high-speed broadband city offices, forget that a large proportion of website users live outside main conurbation areas and still rely on slower internet connections. Not to cater for this sizable percentage of the population is madness.

Trimming down and fighting fit

The biggest mistake for website designers is to use big, bright images to showcase their client's' business or product. Whilst big and bright imagery has its place within web design, it must be used sparingly and cleverly to achieve a fast- loading website.

Modern search engines are monitoring your website visitors' reactions. If a large percentage of your visitors are clicking 'the back button', because of slow loading, then their algorithms will favour a faster loading website above yours.

Think of your website as a Formula One car. Strip it down to basics and functionality, and your website will be faster and slicker. Use big images as a secondary function, detached but linked to the main page. A good example of this is expandable images. These don't affect the web page loading speed unless clicked on.

Third-party functions

A current trend for modern websites is to add third-party functions like Facebook and Twitter feeds, but there are many others. Use these sparingly because these heavily used functions can and do slow the loading speed of your website pages. Test before and after adding these functions to assess the impact, especially at high traffic periods such as evening times.

WEBSITE CONTENT

"This is the most important feature of your website. This is the real meat search engines are looking for when collecting data for their users. So you will be surprised to know that many websites fail the engines' filters by having simple grammar and spelling errors."

Primary and secondary text

Your website users arrive at your pages with various different objectives. Some want to browse and some want information quickly. To cater for both requirements is important in order to keep your 'bounce back rate' low.

Try and break your content down into layers. Place 'In a nutshell' style information at the top, with more detailed explanations towards the bottom. If you can add images to paint a better picture, than keep them small but allow for expansion if required.

Just because you can, does not mean you should

Headings are an important factor in optimizing your pages for search. The standard range of tags available is <h1> to <h6>. Overuse of all or most of these tags can dilute your heading importance.

Try and keep your pages limited to <h1> and <h2> tags only, but if you feel you need more, then consider breaking the content down into additional pages. People confronted by reams of text can find it off-putting, and will quickly reach for the 'back button'.

Write and write some more

Most business owners are fanatical about their particular industry. You have to be to start up and succeed in business, so this is a great opportunity for you to use your enthusiasm to generate new content for your website.

Get a blog - I suggest you set aside 1-2 hours per week starting and updating your blog relating to your industry. This tells the search engines your website is not stagnant and you are possibly a trusted expert in your field.

Check and check again

An early mistake I made in the past was relying on spell check and grammar checkers to publish my content. After a head-scratching period, I found out by sheer chance that the grammar was incomplete at best and completely wrong at worst.

Always check your content in at least two grammar checkers before you publish it. Modern search engines filter out poor quality pages, so if the basic grammar is not up to scratch your pages will sink.

WEBSITE STRUCTURE

"HTML code is what gives your website its structure. As modern search engines continue their drive for quality, this will undoubtedly, if it has not already, shine the spotlight onto structural code."

To comply or not to comply, that is the question

With so many different 'website content management' systems available on the market, it would be easy to think that they all do the same job. In my experience, there are more bad content management systems than there are good ones.

A content management system generates the HTML/PHP or other types of code which gives structure to your website. While your website may look exactly how you want it to look, the underlying HTML/PHP code may be messy at best or wrong at worst.

You can see if your website is 'standards compliant' by going to the 'W3C validator' website and entering a few of your website's page addresses.

Clean, simple and updated coding

The correct and updated 'complaint' structural code will have two important benefits:

- Future-proof your site for search engine quality.
- Simpler and faster page loading.

What to do if your website doesn't comply

Firstly, do not panic. There are many legitimate reasons why a website does not comply, such as third-party additions. After stripping down your pages to basic HTML with your web designer, retest again.

Depending on the severity of the non-compliant pages, you may wish to correct the coding, or for more severe validation problems, updating your 'content management system' may be required.

'Free' comes at a cost

From my experience, 'free websites' or 'free content management systems' can cause sloppy or unnecessary code to be generated. Upgrading your 'content management system' can be done easily, with a free Wordpress installation. However, transferring your existing page information to the new system could cost you.

A consultation with your developer or outsource company will be required.

LINKING

"The internet is by its very nature, an intertwined network of links. Creating links to and from your web pages strengthens the world wide web as well as your site's worldwide appeal."

Roll up, roll up

In times gone by, you would set out your shop or market stall in competition with other traders for the eyes and the ears of the passing public. Absolutely nothing has changed apart from the passing public is now the browsing public.

Word of mouth and a good reputation was and still is the lifeblood of any small or large business, which is why it's still as important today as then to impress.

People who are impressed, whether on quality, price or simply good information, will recommend, talk about and point other people in your direction. This is inbound linking and it's a major factor in modern search engines' ranking signals.

The more links from other quality websites there is that point to yours, the more likely search engines will want to recommend your website to their users.

A two-way street

In an ideal world, lots of people would link their websites, blogs and social networks for you and you'll be on a one-way ticket to search engine heaven. Unfortunately, this is not the case and the search engines may conclude that this is unnatural linking.

Link your website to relevant websites in your niche industry and you will be far less likely to trigger a distrust alert within the search engines' algorithm filters.

Share the love

With the advent of social networks, modern search engines keep a very close eye on what people 'like' and 'tweet' or chat. This is a great way to earn valuable links to your website from your existing customers. The social arena is awash with tips, tricks and recommendations.

Social engagement, if done correctly, can boost your standing with the search engines if you can provide your users with the tools to engage with your site.

Facebook, Tweet Buttons and G+ Buttons are the most commonly used.

Counter-less buttons are recommended, to begin with, then once you have built a reasonable number of 'likes' or '+1's', then encourage more by adding a counter later.

CREATING MOMENTUM

"Like a spinning top, which gives the maximum benefit from a small amount of input at the start, create a website with momentum in mind. This is done with user-generated content and input."

Fuel for your fire

The days of producing a three to a five-page website and expecting success to beat a pathway to your door are over. Successful websites all have one thing in common - user interaction.

If your website looks as though it is unloved, unchanged or has simply stopped growing, then this is a big indicator to search engines that your website is stagnating.

Although this may not be a problem if you only want to be found by your business name (e.g. John Briggs Plumbers), but if you want to seriously compete within the organic search listings for potentially lucrative keywords (e.g. Bathroom fitters in your area), then interactivity within your domain is essential.

Maximum growth with minimum effort

A growing website is a healthier website. With user interaction through comments, forums or social media, search engines will and do, promote websites with evidence of growth.

Most of these interactive social elements can be easily added to most websites, with simple third-party copy and paste services.

Once installed, your website becomes a forum for people to compliment, use as a customer service point or encourage others to use.

All of this generates readable and searchable keyword-rich content for the search engines to offer their users. This then becomes a self-generating entity with only a small amount of moderating needed and large amounts of new visitors to create even more content for you.

Momentum marketing is why so many of the large online businesses encourage their users to rate their products (feedback), comment on products and create customer forums, simply to get maximum website growth for minimum effort.

The starting push

A good website designer or outsource company should be able to implement these additions with minimum effort, then you can simply use the system in your search for new customers and offer rewards to existing customers for singing your praises.

SECURITY

"Prevent your website becoming a victim of its own success by using secure technology. You can shield your website from most of the nasty surprises."

With success comes envy

What people do not warn you about successfulness is the envy that comes with it. The same is true on the internet. Once you are 'top of the pops' for your industry's sought after keywords, your website is in the spotlight, attracting not only new customers but also the wrath of your competitors.

Staying one step ahead of your envious competitors is relatively easy. These have been hard-learned lessons for me, so by reading this book, you have already saved yourself a mountain of headaches, heartache and panic-laden moments.

Negative SEO

Search engine optimisation is pursued to improve website ranking. It can also be used to have the opposite effect, too. Competitors can and do engage in Negative SEO by linking to your website to the bad internet areas. The good news is that this can easily be solved by keeping an eye on your inbound links and using the webmaster tools to 'disavow' unwanted or suspicious looking websites which are linking to your site.

Hacking

This is the most well-known of disruptive behaviours towards websites, but again it can be minimized by asking your hosting provider for an IP address specific FTP access. If your website does receive high volumes of traffic, I would certainly recommend moving hosting with a provider which offers this service.

Even if someone breaks down the username and password, your server will still restrict access because their IP address will be incorrect.

Spoof Emails

You suddenly find out your outgoing e-mails are not reaching their recipients. With investigation, you find out your domain name has been blacklisted for sending spam e-mails.

Finding out that someone has been using your e-mail address for fake e-mails can be irritating at best or could land you in legal trouble at worst. Ask your hosting provider to 'TXT' your domain to prevent outsiders from using your address and your business identity.

CONFIDENCE

"Without user confidence, your website is nothing but a pretty brochure. To realize the full benefits of your website you must portray real trust, expertise and security."

Customer confidence is king

If you are like me, then how many times have you clicked away from a website because your gut feeling swings urgently to distrust?

You are not a business without your customers, so making sure people have full confidence in the security and safety of your website is paramount, in order to turn your search engine success into real sales success.

Professional design versus 'off the shelf'

I have been in the industry long enough to spot an 'off the shelf' website design from twenty paces. A new website visitor will decide, generally within three seconds, whether they are impressed enough to continue further on or reach for the 'back' button.

Before your visitors have read even one word, they already know whether to trust you and your content. Credence comes in many ways, so a well-designed website will help with building trust and authority with the search engines.

Use uniformity to project authority

Uniformity across your website is essential. Wild and wacky designs may be pleasing to the eye, but people may get confused, so keep uniformity across all pages and your website will be received better.

Eye scanner studies show that users generally scan web pages in an 'F' shaped sweep, so put your most popular links on the top left corner of the page.

SSL & validating your domain

Any type of form filling, information-gathering or purchases from your website needs to be SSL secured.

'Secure Server Layer' is an encrypted connection which shows people that you are serious about keeping their details safe.

SSL with the extended validation assures your new visitors that your website is safe and validated and thus giving your website a distinct advantage over non validated sites.

IMAGES

"A picture is worth a thousand words, but on the internet, your pictures may be preventing your words from being read. A frugal but quality approach to images can mean the difference between 'top of the pops' or 'top of the flops."

Rembrandt never intended it this way

In an ideal world, every image and picture on the internet would be as crisp and defined as my 'high definition' television, but the world of the internet is not yet able to carry such high volumes of data.

Images, therefore, have to be used with great care. Bloated websites with high volumes of images do not fare well within the search engine arena. Search engines want to speed up the internet, especially for the huge numbers of users who don't yet have mega broadband speeds.

Minimise everything, leave no image unturned. Reducing your loading speed, therefore, uses your imagery in a more efficient way. Like I said, Rembrandt never intended it this way, but retaining users is more important than wowing them.

Smush-it

There is a little-known service called 'Smush-it' on Yahoo. Use it, Smush-it and reap the benefits. This very clever tool allows you to reduce the size of your images by removing unnecessary Kilobytes from the picture without losing quality.

File formats

To PNG or not to PNG, that is the question. A real test of a knowledgeable website designer is the file formats he/she uses for images. The number of kilobytes between image file formats can differ considerably, thus affecting your load speed.

Photographic images should be saved as PNG. Non-photographic, such as logos, should be saved as GIF file formats.

Quality

Over the years I have received images from clients, which have consisted of magazine cutouts and stolen images from other people's websites, for use in the design of their websites.

The overused 'girl with headset' image or other obviously poor quality imagery is not going to instil confidence in your site. For real quality, original images are paramount if you want your site to be taken seriously.

SEARCH LISTINGS & SEO

"Search engine algorithms automatically assess, organize and filter out the billions of web pages which make up the internet. Website owners can see their website rankings improve, get demoted or disappear from their rankings after algorithmic changes, so it's important to constantly improve the quality of your website."

The race to the top

Every company wants to be at the top of the search engine listing and some businesses pay for the privilege using 'Pay per click' advertisements. This, however, can become very expensive, especially if your business has a lot of competitors.

That then leaves the 'organic' search listings. With the correct criteria, it is technically possible for any website to rank within the first page of search engine listings, thus giving the company a distinct advantage over others.

Algorithms are becoming more intelligent

One of the biggest shake-ups in the SEO was Google's 'Panda and Penguin' algorithm changes. The search engines would probably have readily admitted that their assessments of websites prior to these updates were very 'clunky'.

After the 'Panda and Penguin' changes, the landscape of Google's search listing changed forever. The other popular search engines are likely to follow with this more 'intelligent' approach to assessing and ranking websites in their search pages.

Quality websites share the same characteristics as other quality websites - a very black and white issue - and it is these characteristics which the new algorithms look for when assessing and filtering websites from their listings.

Google's website guidelines are a good place to begin to understand the mind of a modern search engine and will stand your business in good stead for any future algorithmic changes as all of the popular search companies continue to strive to give their users a better quality service.

Search engine optimisation

SEO or 'search engine optimisation' is an industry which tweaks websites in order to gain technical advantages over other websites. Firstly, this is an industry which has many more bad practitioners than good.

An inexperienced company or person can inflict more damage than improvement if done incorrectly. Choose wisely and always get written confirmation of their intended work schedule, if you decide to outsource this type of service.

BAD OPTIMISATION

"Get it right and the rewards can be fabulous for your business, but get it wrong and the consequences can be fatal for your business."

Too many cooks spoil the broth

As a veteran of the 'search engine optimisation' industry, I see on a regular basis the amount of information available to people on the subject of SEO. A wealth of information on a subject should be a positive thing, but unfortunately, the super-fast pace in which search engines change their criteria leaves 98% of that information:

1. **Outdated**, because techniques which may have worked in

previous years are now a 'poisoned chalice'.

2. **Untrue**, because nobody actually knows what signals Google and others look for, so much of what you read about SEO is guesswork.

3. **Dangerous**, because SEO techniques come in two classes - 'black hat' and 'white hat'. If you stumble across and implement any 'black hat' techniques, the search engines could ban you from their listings altogether.

Advice read on the internet should always be taken with a pinch of salt, and any techniques you or an outsource company undertake should always be tested first then retested.

Run for the hills

There is a minefield of bad SEO companies all shouting the same message, "We can get your business to the #1 position on Google", or "We work in partnership with Google".

Does that sound familiar? The truth is that nobody or any SEO company can guarantee success. They can only work within the guidelines. Trying to get you to the top of the search engines with long-tail keywords that people would never use is not good SEO.

Real search engine optimisation

Real search engine optimisation is a long-term strategy. No overnight success will come from today's SEO strategies, but when done correctly you can watch your 'user rate' rise, your 'bounce rate' lower and your 'search ranking' climb the ladder steadily to your 'page 1' goal.

Link schemes and keyword densities will not help your website. Only quality content, continued growth and user approval will see your website succeed.

QUALITY SIGNALS

"You may think your website users are 'your' users. They are actually the search engine's users and they will continue to send their users to websites which they view as good quality. Convincing their algorithms that your website is a quality website is what good 'search engine optimisation' is all about."
Black and white

The big search engine companies are as secretive and protective over their algorithms, as the 'Colonel's secret recipe (aka Kentucky Fried Chicken)' and Coca Cola's commercial ingredients, so walk away from any person or company that says differently.

Of the billions of websites currently available, the quality one's share many good characteristics. Making sure your website has these 'good' characteristics will improve your chances of not only reaching the top positions of the search pages but keeping it there too.

General characteristics of a quality website

- Correct grammar and spelling.
- Fast loading.
- Outbound links to other quality, subject- relevant websites.
- Lots of inbound links from other quality and authoritative websites.
- Links to social network chatter.
- Websites hosted on a long-term domain name.
- Websites on reliable and country relevant hosting company.
- Websites on an authoritative domain name.
- Continually growing websites.
- Modern website HTML code.
- Validated website code via W3C standards.
- Contact details
- Websites with SSL with for user security.
- Websites with user interactions.

- Websites with extended validation.
- Websites on quality website directories such a DMOZ/BOTW.
- Websites with low 'Bounceback' rates.
- Websites with higher user retention and page views.
- Websites with relevant titles and content.

The search engines are eager for everyone to improve their websites and give out lots of information to help you do this. My 50 website improvements checklist is available at the back of this book.

In addition, check out Google's 'Head of Search Quality and Webspam', Matt Cutts updates, who answers a lot of webmasters' questions on his blog.

ON-SITE ADVERTS

"Many business-oriented websites include advertisements as part of their revenue stream, but this could be having a detrimental effect on your website's ranking position."

Temptation to monetize

Thinking of ways to add content to a website can sometimes be hard for many people. Adding third-party advertisements to your website to fill space and also earn you extra revenue can sometimes be tempting. Please be aware that this can sometimes be a poison chalice to some websites.

If you do decide to go down this route for your website, then use it sparingly.

A search engine's point of view

We have all encountered websites where most of the screen is filled with advertisements, and although the search engines don't have a problem with adverts, they do have a problem with the links that are not disclosed as being 'paid for'.

Always use the: rel="no follow" on any outgoing links which have been placed for monetary gain. Failure to do so may see your website penalised.

A user's point of view

Since the early days of the internet, 'pop up', embedded or flashy adverts have been annoying, causing most users to eventually become blind to them. If the main objective of your site is to sell your own products, generate leads or promote your own business, then this type of additional content may be doing more harm than good.

Performance

Additional images and third-party inclusions add additional loading speed onto your pages. Weighing up the value of such adverts and the consequential additional load speed should be a priority. If you are not sure, then I recommend 'split testing' your content, with and without advert space to make sure your current monetization strategy is truly benefitting you.

Bounce

By adding adverts on your site, you run the risk of a noticeable percentage of your website users 'bouncing' away from your website to your advertiser's website. Algorithms will detect this as a negative signal - food for thought.

ALGORITHMIC EVENTS

"Every once in awhile, search engines make changes

to their algorithms which have impacts on their search listings. If you or the person in charge of your website is following SEO trends on the internet, then you may be leaving your website open to be 'punished' with the next algorithm change or tweak."

Don't feel sheepish by following SEO trends

Ever since the 1990s, the 'search engine optimisation' industry has come up with many variations and manipulative ways to try and outsmart the search engines and benefit from higher search rankings.

This has led to millions of website owners or developers following the latest SEO trends to gain a competitive advantage over others.

The problem with following SEO trends is that millions of others and Google will also be following such ways to manipulate their core business. For this reason, you can guarantee that the search engines are smarter than any self-proclaimed 'SEO guru' and will inevitably tune their algorithms to filter out those manipulative websites.

Algorithmic victims

If your website has fallen prey to recent algorithm changes, then, unfortunately, you will need firstly, to find out why and secondly, how to recover. There are two types of removals from the search listing, Manual and Algorithmic exclusions.

The manual exclusion will require you to clean your website of any manipulative SEO that may have been done in the past and submit a 'reconsideration request' for re-inclusion. During this reconsideration request, you must be honest and admit your website's SEO faults and give a meaningful apology.

Algorithmic exclusions are easier to recover from because you may only need to change or remove your manipulative SEO strategies and wait for the next algorithm update to roll out.

An upfront and honest discussion are required with the person or people responsible for your website, in order to get to the reason behind your exclusion. Some common manipulative practices are:

- Link wheels or linking networks/schemes.
- Paid links.
- Keyword stuffing.
- Duplicate and content scraping from other websites.
- Inconsistent quality.
- Cloaking and doorway pages.

CONTENT DELIVERY NETWORKS

""Shipping your website data around the world for international audiences will leave your website slow for people in other countries. A Content Delivery Network is a lot like having a warehouse in each time-zone for the distribution of your website content, for a better experience for international users."

A global solution to a global technology

CDN or 'Content Delivery Networks' is a collection of high-speed data centres spread out across each continent which delivers your website content without having to send it across the globe.

These are what larger global companies such as Google, Facebook and eBay use to give a better and faster website experience to all their global users. You don't have to be a large sized company to take advantage and gain the benefits of a truly global website.

A good idea for small websites too

You may notice in your analytics data that not everyone viewing your website is in the same country as your business. Having a CDN network will give everyone a better user experience.

As modern search engines are continually analyzing users' responses wherever they may live, it makes sense to give a faster website experience to everyone not just local users to improve your SEO strategy.

The benefits

Most business websites use a single hosting company to deliver the images and additional files which make up a website. With a copy of your website assets in every corner of the globe, search engines will not punish your website for the small or large percentage of users that may discover your website and live abroad.

As previously discussed, search engine algorithms are making 'site speed' an important factor in assessing websites in today's competitive search results, and the likelihood that companies like Google are testing your website from their own eight worldwide data centres.

Test and test again

Having a website which works well in every corner of the globe and on every media interface such as older browsers, newer browsers, mobile phones and tablet devices is paramount for a truly successful website.

Keep your users happy and search engines will soon recognize and reward your efforts.

COOKIE LAW

"You could be forgiven for not knowing this, but the law has changed this year, requiring websites in the European Union to declare to its users which type

cookies are used."
Cookies, cookies everywhere

A cookie is a piece of data which has the ability to track users at the extreme end of the scale or simply to aid a website's inner workings at the benevolent end.

A guide to cookie policy

This guide will help you determine your legal obligations. However, you should always consult with your original website designer, who will be able to confirm your website cookie status.

Cookies come in many different forms, which can make the issue of compliance complicated. Some cookies are used for the performance of the website, and others can gather data about users and their habits, with many other types in between, namely:

- Strictly necessary & performance cookies.
- Functional cookies
- Targeting cookies.

Before you can categorise the cookies your website uses, you first need to detect them and analyse them. Cookies can be broken down into 4 categories:

Zero compliance cookies - Always first party and non-persistent. These include functional navigation and user session cookies for shopping carts.

Low compliance risk - Always first party and may be persistent. These cookies include accessibility options for visually impaired users and analytics cookies.

Medium risk cookies - Usually first party and persistent. These might be used to store personally identifiable information, or limited cross-site tracking, in order to present content that is based on previous visits.

High compliance risk - These are mainly used to track and record visitor interests without prior consent and aggregated this data for use by third parties. (Normally advertisers).

TO CONCLUDE

"The internet has an infinite number of ways of doing things. Website creation and the search engines that assess them are still evolving, so there is no right or wrong way of doing things. The recommendations contained within this book are compiled from experience with knowledge of what is required to stay on the right side of the search engine algorithms and hopefully make the job of outranking your competitors easier to achieve."

Rome wasn't built in a day

Web marketing is a lot like entering a robot war competition. Give your website a fighting chance by following these important technical alterations and proven strategies, to compete in your chosen field of expertise.

Algorithm updates

The latest round of Google changes has left a lot of businesses feeling unhappy this year. Alterations to algorithms have seen business websites fall in Google's listings, especially those that depended heavily on SEO (search engine optimisation) services.

Search engines have made it clear that the changes it makes to clear "Webspam" from its listings will continue, so those who may not have been affected yet may still see their current positions fall or even delisted later.

In the still-evolving world of the search engines, websites which "over optimise" or overdo SEO, rather than just create brilliant content will be most affected. To avoid the risk of being penalised, it's imperative you follow Google's guidelines.

Make sure you are up to date with the latest SEO techniques, as these are forever changing, such as keyword stuffing, which is now frowned upon by the search engines.

While 'Search Engine Optimisation' principles can help a business website to be better placed in search listings, there are plenty of "under-optimized" websites that are excellent and would benefit from some search optimisation alterations.

The most significant up and coming alterations to new algorithms will be the use of social network signals. Therefore the necessity of keeping up a strong social community on your website is crucial.

These types of changes are easy to implement and once they are in place, they will leave your business website more competitive for years to come.

SIX MONTH IMPROVEMENT CHALLENGE

"Web marketing is like entering a robot war competition. Give your website a fighting chance by following these important technical alterations and proven strategies, to compete in your chosen field of expertise."

An honest assessment of your website

Current website hits: …………….... (Per week/month)   Bounce rate: ……………....

Do you get enquiries: Many / Moderately / Rarely / Never
*Number of enquiries: (Per week/month)

The target number of enquiries: ……………....

Website load speed: ……………....

Number of pages: ……………....

Keywords researched:

Create a list of keywords and key phrases and note your current positions. This will help you compare changes in your positions after making any positive changes to your website:

CHECKLIST

50 ways to improve your business website.

"The techniques illustrated here can help your website improve over the next 6 months. Search engines tweak their algorithms approximately every three to six months. Just by making two of these changes per week will mean the next time the search engine scans your website, they will see a much healthier website than before."

For those with limited time factors, by delegating only 2 of these changes per week, then your website will be fighting fit within approximately six months.

"It's not the size of the man in the fight...it's the size of the fight in the man"
Napoleon Bonaparte (1769-1821)

50 ways to improve your business website

1. Get the right mindset:

Focusing on improving your website will bring great satisfaction when you see the results, but this will be a long-term push for the summit, and my checklist will assist with every step of the way. Are you truly up for the challenge?

2. Website load speed:

Loading speed is an increasingly important factor. You can measure your website speed and receive tips to reduce it if necessary:

http://www.webpagetest.org/

Something as simple as changing your hosting company to one with more modern servers, or more complicated issues relating to your website. Use the 'web page test' tool to see if your website can do better.

3. Image optimisation:

A major factor in load speed is your image size and file format. You can reduce load speed by minimizing image sizes and using Yahoo's 'Smush' facility:

http://smushit.com/

4. Image file type:

Make sure your non-photographic images are delivered as a GIF file format and your JPG files are minimized as much as possible. Think about using expandable images or thumbnails if you want to show higher quality images.

5. Amount of images:

Websites crammed full of images undoubtedly are the cause of slow loading. Can you reduce the number of images, and still get the same message? Can you reduce the sizes of some or all of your images?

Think of your website as a lean, mean sprinting machine without images. Then the more image 'weight' or Kilobytes you add will (like a fully laden car) reduce performance.

6. Titles and meta tags:

Compose your most important keywords in your title tag with no more than 70 characters. Get rid of the 'keywords' meta tag because search engines ignore them nowadays. Use a nice, keyword-laden description tag which may be used in the listings.

<meta name="description" content="Add your description." />

Additionally, use the 'author tag' because it is becoming increasingly important that authors of web pages are disclosed.

<meta name=author content="Joe Bloggs" />

As search engines have many data centres across the globe, the 'language' meta tag helps send your web pages to their correct geographical audience.

<meta http-equiv="content-language" content="en-gb">

Social meta tags are used to convey important information about a web page if that webpage gets linked via a social network site, thus increasing the SEO value of that link. Add your keyword- laden information in the content brackets:

<meta property='og:locale' content='en_GB'/>
<meta property='og:title' content='/>
<meta property='og:description' content="/>
<meta property='og:url' content="/>
<meta property='og:site_name' content=''/>
<meta property='og:type' content="/>
<meta property='og:image' content="/>
<meta name="twitter:card" content="summary">
<meta name="twitter:site" content="">
<meta name="twitter:creator" content="">
<meta name="twitter:title" content="">
<meta name="twitter:" ">
<meta name="twitter:url" content="">

7. Content per page:

When you are writing new pages or articles, try to make each one over 600 words. Articles with fewer words are more likely to be discarded by search engines, simply because an expert on any subject will be able to write more than 600 words on a particular subject. That's a search engine's viewpoint.

8. Prominent Phone No:

Many of your website users don't want to read a whole web page to find a phone number.

Make it easy for them by having it in a prominent place. Ask incoming telephone enquiries where they found your phone number to assess your site's success.

9. Grammar/spelling:

Bad spelling and grammar are easily detectable by search engines. Check and double-check content using facilities such as:

http://www.grammarly.com/

If you have a forum or comments system attached to your website, always moderate and grammar check the incoming content before approving their full publication.

10. Privacy policy:

Search engines view websites with the proper 'terms and conditions' with greater professionalism than websites with none.

Put a "privacy policy" at the foot of every page. It not only helps your users find your legal standpoint but also shows the search engines your professionalism.

A separate page with your 'cookie law' obligations and other terms of use is common practice.

11. Plagiarism issues:

Many other website owners copy other people's website content to use as their own. Duplicate content is easily detectable by search engines nowadays, so protect your content.

Use anti-plagiarism regularly and serve '*Digital Millennium Copyright Act*' (DMCA) notices to those who do steal your content.

http://www.copyscape.com/

Claim authorship of all your pages by using the:

<meta name="author" content="John Smith"> tag and *rel="author"* within a footer link, linking to your 'Google profile' account.

12. Webmaster tools/verify:

Join Google and Bing webmaster's tools service. Verify your website ownership through them. There is also very valuable statistical information given on your website's performance once set-up.

Verifying your website's authenticity through 'Webmaster Tools' will give it a more trustworthy image. This can be done easily using a meta tag:

1. *On the Webmaster Tools Home page, click the **Manage Site** button next to the site you want and then click **Verify this site**.*
2. *If **HTML tag** is not visible on the **recommended method** tab, click the **alternate methods** tab.*
3. *Select **HTML tag**, and follow the steps on your screen.*
4. *Once you've added the tag to your home page, click **Verify**.*

13. Sitemap:

To help the search engines find all your pages, create a sitemap. A simple generator tool can help:

http://www.xml-sitemaps.com/

 Once created, submit your sitemap to Google and Bing.

Search engine's spider bots continually crawl and gather data about your website and this will help them do just that.

Provide an HTML sitemap for your visitor and an XML version for the search engines.

14. HTML validation:

Your website is made up of structural code called HTML (Hypertext

Markup Language). Depending on the original creator, your website may or may not validate. Check your website validates at

http://validator.w3.org/

Third-party additions on your website may affect validation, so always validate without third-party attachments for a clearer view of potential issues.

15. Check browser rendering:

Poor validation can sometimes cause issues with different browsers. Always check the rendering of your pages if you make changes to the structure of the site.

If your website is modern, the CSS code (Cascading Style Sheets) makes up most of the structure of your website. Some CSS codes do not render websites equally on different web browsers. Check your website in:

- Google Chrome, 6,7,8,9
- Apple's Safari browsers
- Firefox
- Internet Explorer, 5, 6,7,8,9

16. Call to action:

Many websites fail to put a 'call to action' in a prominent place. If you want your users to fill in a form, see a sales page, or any other course of action, you must make sure they can find their way.

17. Relative linking:

Check for a non-**http://** internal links. Always use the full **http://** and your full domain in all in-site linking.

Having pages that do and don't use this prefix can dilute the effectiveness of your website.

<img src=http://www.yoursite.co.uk/hello-world.htm **(YES)**
<img src=hello-world.htm **(NO)**

18. Distractions:

A common mistake made by many websites is information overload for new users. On-site adverts distracting and taking your users away from your website could have a negative effect on your own ability to generate leads/sales.

Too many adverts spoil the broth. Simplify your pages and see more positive user statistics.

19. Stay fresh:

When did you last add more interesting textual information to your site? Growing your website over the long-term will help. A blog is the most common form of updating websites.

Search engines will have a much more positive view of your site if it is regularly updated with fresh quality content, than more stagnant sites.

20. Best of the Web:

Enroll your website on this paid-for directory because they vet all listed websites, Search engines give additional link credit to websites who are listed:

http://botw.org/

21. Yahoo directory:

Enroll your website on this paid-for directory because this site vets websites, search engines give link credit to websites who are listed:
http://dir.yahoo.com/

22. DMOZ directory:

Enroll your website on this paid-for directory. A free directory, but because this site vets listed websites, SE's give link credit to websites who are listed:

http://www.dmoz.org/

23. Google Places:

Add your business to Google's local listings. Google gives priority to its own local listings for local search queries:

http://www.google.com/places/

24. Google Merchant:

If you sell products, then you can add your products to a spreadsheet and upload them to Google's servers, which will instantly add them to their product listings:

http://www.google.co.uk/merchants/

25. Like for like:

This is an incoming link which acquires strategy from similar or content related websites to your own. Links of useful resources relating to your industry are helpful.

A list of websites linking to your website can be viewed on Google's webmaster tools, and you can check your competitors' incoming link profile at *http://www.backlinkwatch.com/*

26. Add comments:

Enabling your website users to interact and respond to your content will create a fresh, updated website content with little effort from yourself.

Always moderate the quality of user-generated content and grammar check before approving others' content. A self-generating website is a healthier website when done correctly: *http://www.disqus.com/*

27. News and views:

Write about your expertise, update industry-related news regularly and add an interesting spin to your subject matter. This will allow people to comment and will add additional, all- important search engine-friendly content to your site for free.

The most common and easy to use software for publishing news and updates is Wordpress, which has a choice of plugs to add additional functionality to your pages.

Set aside two hours of your week or your staff's week for writing a news blog or an article of interest. Try to keep updated as often as possible and the search engines will love it.

28. Breadcrumbs:

Breadcrumbs are the link of links which show at the top of each page to show how deep you have gone on a website or through a process such as a form filling. An example would be:

Home > Category >. This is the page title of a web page

Adding links, so that your users can find their way around your site more easily also gives additional benefits of allowing the search engines to find content more easily.

29. Signature and date:

Always sign your blog news with the date published and the author's signature. This protocol is essential for search engines to take your articles seriously. Author-named pages will rank higher than author-less pages.

A profile page for each author/authors, with additional pictures and a writing done with expertise, will add a touch more professionalism to your website. Outbound links to accredited or professional bodies also will enhance the professionalism of such pages.

30. Social sharing:

Allow people to share, follow and give your site a boost.

These social signals, as search engines call them, will show that your website is 'like-able' and thus worth directing search engine users to.

If you use your own 'Like', 'G+', or tweet buttons, to name a few, then remember you will need additional images which may slow your site down. Third-party software can do this easily: *http://www.addthis.com/*

31. Google +:

Open a Google+ account and add links to your new article pages when they are published. Interested people will add you or your business to their 'circles' and this information is then relayed within the actual search engine listings.

"Joe Bloggs has 568 followers in his circles."

Make sure you triangulate your rel="author" links to your Google pages and your web pages, which will authenticate your authorship.

In addition, you can set-up a business web page through this account. Use this to add additional related content and harness the large amounts of users found on this network.

32. Facebook and Twitter:

Open both Facebook and Twitter accounts, then add links to your new article pages when published and interact with your followers.

In addition, you can set-up a business web page through your Facebook account. Just like the Google+ page, use this to add additional related content and harness the large amounts of users found on these networks.

33. Content Delivery Network:

After you have found a suitable CDN provider, it only requires a quick tweak of the .htaccess file, add a CNAME alternative with your DNS provider and alterations of your image and resource file links will enable your site to be truly global:

<img src=http://yourwebsite.cdn.com/images/image.gif />

34. Google +1:

Add a Google +1 button to every web page. Each additional '+1' received tells Google you have just had a 'thumbs up' from your users. Sites with more '+1's'will have a more positive influence on the search engines than those without.

Search engines will increasingly add more weight to these types of signals in the future, so start collecting now to receive the full benefits of these social signals.

35. Ease of use?

If your site is designed to collect sales leads or sell products, then get a few friends or family members to test the usability. I promise you, you will get a good insight into how your users struggle to navigate. Use this information to improve your site structure.

36. Easy on the eye?

Aesthetics are relative to each individual person, but if your site design and colour scheme are eye-watering, gaudy or dated looking, then you could almost certainly be losing sales.

A clean, conservative and modern design can improve sales, user interaction and give improved analytical data which ultimately reflect on your search engine ranking position.

37. Video Introduction:

This is entirely optional but useful for keeping people on your web pages for longer. Search engines take account of the amount of time that people spend on particular pages and rank accordingly.

A good and interesting video or videos can be found on the YouTube network, giving extra interest to your content.

If you do decide to invest in video production for your website, always use a professional cameraman and a professional editor. A badly shot and edited video will have people reaching for the 'back button' and having entirely the opposite effect you intended.

38. External linking policy:

Choose your outgoing links wisely. Only link to good authority and related websites, which can add value to your site. Linking out to bad internet neighbourhoods can have a detrimental effect on your rankings.

Linking schemes and link wheel programs, once popular in the search engine optimization industry, now have a detrimental effect on the websites that used them.

Think quality over quantity.

39. Internal link structure:

Use keywords in links. Make all your pages accessible from every page of your website. Do not use image-based links, especially 'rollovers', as these increase loading speed. Always use CSS to style your links.

Full "http://" values are necessary to prevent dilution of your pages' influence. Use 2-4 external and internal links within the main content if possible.

Make your link colours bright and easily recognised. Hiding links with the same colour specifications as the surrounding text will get your website penalized.

Put your useful content links above lesser useful pages.

Avoid lengthy lists of links if possible because this can confuse your visitors.

Don't use the 'title' facility within the links <a href="" /> because this can be seen as keyword stuffing by search engines.

40. Forms:

Have you ever intended to fill in an online form, then being put off by the length of it? Long winded forms are a big turnoff to users, so get the basics and if necessary get the additional information from the customer via a phone call.

Having problems with spam. Use Google's ReCaptcha service: *http://www.google.com/recaptcha/captcha*

41. SSL:

Secure Server Layer (SSL) instils user confidence in your website by encrypting your user's data.

The padlock in the browser is essential if you are to know with confidence that your website users are not 'clicking away' as a result of not having it.

Extended SSL validation can help your business in the search engines too. Expensive but worth it.

42. Install Tynt:

Plagiarism is rife on the internet. You may not be able to stop it, but you can use it to your benefit. Tynt is a very clever service which tracks, analyses and adds a link to your web page that your content has been stolen from.

This gives your website credit and a link back to your page:
http://www.tynt.com/

43. Font:

I have had many a debate about font sizing on websites, but my gut feeling is that small font (10 pixels) on a website's main content can be off-putting to older or visually impaired users.

"Should I go and find my reading glasses or click back and find another website?"

A minimum of 14-pixel sizing is recommended. Colour contrast may also contribute to eye tiredness, so keeping your main text font to a less eye-watering hue colour, will allow users to stay on your pages for longer.

44. Cookie law compliance:

1. Does your website collect analytical data? (Low risk)
2. Does your website remember previous users? (Medium risk)
3. Does your website use social network buttons? (Low to medium risk)
4. Does your website have third-party advertising or data storage? (High risk)

Low risk – Add to your privacy policy page an addition regarding your cookie policy.
Implied consent can be used adding in most cases.

Low to medium risk – A privacy policy update may be sufficient, or a customer notification may be best if multiple forms data collection is used.

Medium risk – A customer notification upon entering the website is required. The customer's consent will need to be recorded in a database.

High risk – A customer notification is required. For a full compliance service.

http://*www.cookielaw.org*

45. A number of pages:

A number of pages a website has are a major factor in the assessment of your website by search engines. A good quality website with 25 pages will be more likely to outrank a similar website with says only 10 pages. Try to create a fresh page once a week.
Curating news and related articles are the most common way of doing this.

46. Old or altered web page URL's

Search engines have great memories. If you have discontinued a web page for whatever reason, then you must add a robots.txt file within your root directory. This will tell the search engines not to list that page anymore.

Simply removing a page, will create a 404 error message which looks bad for your site:

*User-agent: ** *
allow: /index, follow/
Disallow: /

For your site users, you can use a 301 in a '.htaccess' file, which will send users to a new page:

Redirect permanent /old http://www.yourwebsite.co.uk/new

47. Be an "honest" rather than a "deceptive" website:

As my mum used to say, "Honesty is the best policy" and this has never been so true when trying to create a successful but long-term successful website.

Over the years, the 'search engine optimisation' industry has come up with so many ways to fool and deceive the search engine's into giving them a top position. Since then most of these websites have been 'rumbled' and sent back down the listings or filtered out altogether by the new generation of search algorithms.

If you do read on the internet about a new way to trick the search engines (and there are many), you can guarantee that the search engines have read it too, and will deal with offenders on their next algorithm tweak and update.

48. Provide a better user experience:

In the earlier days of my career, I had fallen into the trap of creating websites that 'WOW' people over websites that just get the job done.

Although a good design is important, it should never be at the expense of functionality. A still all too common mistake made by designers today. If your users 'don't get it' then your flashy designs are wasted.

Think about the Ebay, Facebook and Amazon. Great examples of functionality over design. Keep it simple and your users will 'get it' and use it.

Provide satisfactory answers for users.

Selling or generating leads for your business comes as a secondary consequence of your users looking for information. Providing the correct and easy to understand information should be a priority of any business website.

The truth is people don't care how your business got started. They care only for the information they seek. If you cannot provide that information, then your users will find a website that can.

Your website content must reflect this need, and if done correctly, then your sales or leads will increase as a result of your improved content.

49. Schema markup

Schema markup allows you to specify which are the important details on your website.

This is especially useful for e-commerce or database websites which search engine spiders find hard to distinguish which is the most relevant information.

In some cases, the markup can be useful for getting your information on the search engine listings for certain search queries: http://schema.org/

50. Mobile-friendly

The 'smartphone' market has changed everything. People are using their phones to access the internet more and more. If your website is still not 'mobile-friendly', then you will already be losing people to the dreaded 'back button'.

Mobile-friendly websites can be remarkably easy to implement. A good website designer will be able to 'mobilise' an averagely sized website within a day.

Don't let the marching tide of 'smartphone' use, erode your website's effectiveness.

Patience

Go and treat yourself. Search engine algorithm filters are updated every 3-6 months. Your website will be re-evaluated and re-positioned in the search listings accordingly.

The last word

"Neither I or others have control over the results of search engines; I recommend the above-mentioned alterations and strategies; which from experience will improve your page rankings in the search engine results pages.

The continued long-term, amendments, both on-site and socially, are key indicators to the search engines, that your website is a goldmine of information, therefore, more trustworthy and more relevant to its users.

Quality control of published information is essential in the virtual world, just as in the real world.

Create expert content, but more importantly, love what you do, which your readers will pick up on and engage with you more."

Stuart Lovatt

About the author

"The love for web design was instant, but the search optimisation knowledge was acquired through many years of trial and error. I currently have 14 years proven SEO success."

After being accepted to work within the design team of a large ISP (Internet Service Provider), in 1998 when Google was being spawned out of a garage, I first learned the do's and don'ts of making websites appear higher up, the then, Altavista, Yahoo and Lycos search engines.

www.yourimagematters.co.uk/about-stuart-lovatt.htm

www.ingramcontent.com/pod-product-compliance
Lightning Source LLC
Chambersburg PA
CBHW041146050326
40689CB00001B/507